Let's Sort,
It's a Real Sport!

Tracy Kompelien

Consulting Editors, Diane Craig, M.A./Reading Specialist
and Susan Kosel, M.A. Education

ABDO
Publishing Company

Published by ABDO Publishing Company, 4940 Viking Drive, Edina, Minnesota 55435.

Credits
Edited by: Pam Price
Curriculum Coordinator: Nancy Tuminelly
Cover and Interior Design and Production: Mighty Media
Photo Credits: AbleStock, Photodisc, ShutterStock, Wewerka Photography

Library of Congress Cataloging-in-Publication Data

Kompelien, Tracy, 1975-
   Let's sort, it's a real sport! / Tracy Kompelien
   p. cm. -- (Math made fun)
   ISBN 10 1-59928-539-8 (hardcover)
   ISBN 10 1-59928-540-1 (paperback)

   ISBN 13 978-1-59928-539-9 (hardcover)
   ISBN 13 978-1-59928-540-5 (paperback)
   1. Group theory--Juvenile literature. 2. Categories (Mathematics)--Juvenile literature. 3. Similarity
judgment--Juvenile literature. I. Title. II. Series.

QA174.5.K66 2007
512'.2--dc22

                                                           2006012559

SandCastle Level: Transitional

SandCastle™ books are created by a professional team of educators, reading specialists, and content developers
around five essential components—phonemic awareness, phonics, vocabulary, text comprehension, and fluency—to assist
young readers as they develop reading skills and strategies and increase their general knowledge. All books are written,
reviewed, and leveled for guided reading, early reading intervention, and Accelerated Reader® programs for use in
shared, guided, and independent reading and writing activities to support a balanced approach to literacy instruction.
The SandCastle™ series has four levels that correspond to early literacy development. The levels help teachers and parents
select appropriate books for young readers.

| **Emerging Readers** | **Beginning Readers** | **Transitional Readers** | **Fluent Readers** |
| (no flags) | (1 flag) | (2 flags) | (3 flags) |

These levels are meant only as a guide. All levels are subject to change.

To sort

is to separate objects by kind or class.

Words used to sort:
alike
classify
different
group
same
similar

This 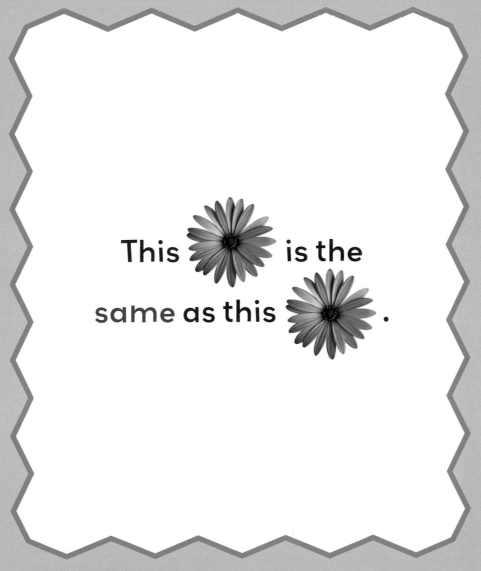 is the same as this .

The  and the are alike.

The  is similar to the .

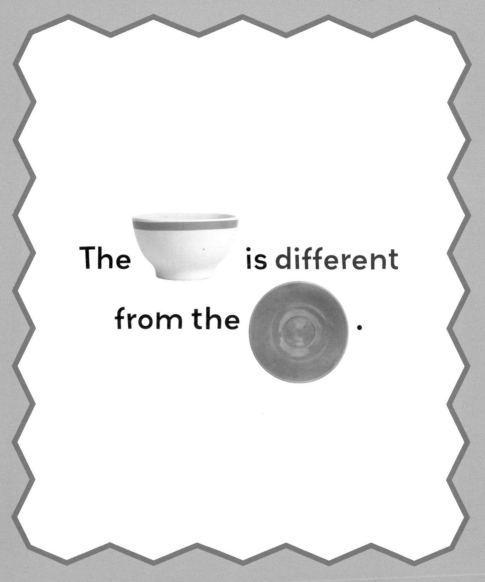

The is different

from the .

The  and the are not alike.

The and the

can be classified

as the same.

Let's Sort, It's a Real Sport!

Mort is learning to sort.

He starts to see

which are alike.

That's the key.

I will start
by looking at
the size and
type of ball!

twelve
12

Mort sorts by color, size, and type. Some balls are blue, some have a stripe.

I am going to start sorting by grouping the balls that have similar sizes.

fourteen
14

Mort is such a sport.
He has finished
doing the sort!

Next I sort the balls so that they are grouped by type.

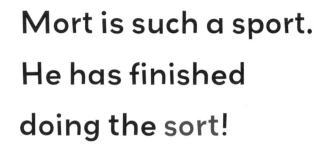

Sorting Every Day!

When Cort puts away her clothes, she sorts them into piles of the same type.

This type of shirt is a T-shirt.

eighteen
18

Cort will organize her ribbons. She will put similar colors together.

I will group the ribbons that look alike.

twenty
20

At the grocery store, fruit is organized by grouping items that are alike.

They are also sorted by color!

Can you think of things that you like to sort?

I like to sort my candy and share it with my friends. I also like to sort the socks in my drawer by color and size.

Glossary

alike – almost the same.

classify – to put things in groups according to their characteristics.

different – not the same.

group – to put items together.

not alike – not the same.

same – identical in every way.

similar – having characteristics in common.